All A

by Lisa C. Moran

HOUGHTON MIFFLIN HARCOURT
School Publishers

PHOTOGRAPHY CREDITS: Cover Carolyn A. McKeone /Photo Researchers, Inc. 1 Tom McHugh/Photo Researchers, Inc. 2 Alvin E. Staffan/Photo Researchers, Inc. 3 Alvin E. Staffan/Photo Researchers, Inc. 4 © JUERGEN & CHRISTINE SOHNS/ Animals Animals-Earth Scenes. 5 © JUERGEN & CHRISTINE SOHNS/Animals Animals-Earth Scenes. 6 Tom McHugh/Photo Researchers, Inc. 7 Tom McHugh/Photo Researchers, Inc. 8 STEPHEN DALTON/Minden Pictures. 9 Carolyn A. McKeone/ Photo Researchers, Inc. 10 © George Steinmetz/CORBIS.

Printed in China

ISBN-13: 978-0-547-02159-1
ISBN-10: 0-547-02159-3

5 6 7 8 0940 18 17 16 15 14 13 12
4500345298

Introduction

Mice live all over the world. Mice can live in the frozen cold of the Arctic. They can live in the fiery heat of the desert. Mice are tiny, but they are also amazing. Let's meet some mice.

Mice can live almost anywhere that has food and water.

The House Mouse

The house mouse is a rodent. *Rodent* is the scientific name for animals that gnaw, or chew. Rodents gnaw with their front teeth. Their front teeth are always growing so they gnaw to keep them from getting too big.

Mice sometimes gnaw on things like leather and wood.

House mice are very small. They are six to eight inches long from nose to tail. They are about one inch tall. A mouse's small size helps it in an emergency. A mouse can hide in a very small place.

Mice are very strong for their size. They can climb. They can jump. They can even swim.

Mice use their tails to help them balance as they climb.

Mice use their paws to pick up food.

House mice use their senses to live. Mice have very good senses of smell and hearing. Mice use their big noses and ears to find their way around. They use their whiskers to feel. Whiskers tell a mouse immediately if it can fit into a hole or not.

The Life of a Mouse

Some mice get food from people. House mice eat seeds and nuts. They like cereal and pasta. Mice love sweets.

Mice live inside and outside. They live outside in warm weather. They move inside when it is cold. Mice like to live within house walls and barns.

Mice like to make their nests out of warm things, like grasses and paper.

These pups will leave their mother after four weeks.

A family of mice grows very quickly. A baby mouse is called a pup. A pair of mice may have forty pups in one year.

Mice live a short life. Wild mice live between one and two years. A mouse is an adult when it is only two months old. Mice like to live near people.

In ancient times, mice may have lived with humans. These prehistoric mice lived in caves, too. People got rid of mice then, too.

Mice face many dangers in the wild. Many animals hunt mice for food. Owls and snakes eat mice. Foxes and coyotes also eat mice.

You can see a mouse panicking when it sees a cat.

Pet mice can be many colors.

Some people think mice are horrifying. But others keep mice as pets. Pet mice may live as long as six years. They are fun to watch in their cages.

Scientists also use mice. They study the mice in labs. They study mice to learn about things that make us sick.

Conclusion

Maybe you like mice. Maybe you don't. You may find mice mysterious and interesting. You may think mice are pests. Either way, mice are everywhere. It seems that mice are here to stay.

How to Keep Pet Mice

- Have more than one mouse.
- Give your mice a large cage and plenty of food and water.
- Add wood shavings, grass, or hay.
- Add toys, too.
- Play with your mice!

Responding

TARGET VOCABULARY **Word Builder**

Make a word web around the word mysterious. What other words mean the same as mysterious? Copy the web and add more words.

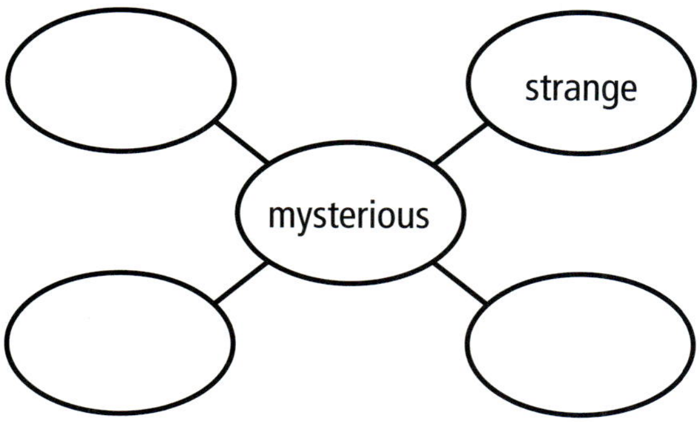

Write About It

Text to Self Do you find it mysterious that people want mice as pets? Tell why or why not. Compare having a mouse to having another kind of pet. Use words from the web in your writing.

TARGET VOCABULARY

ancient	mysterious
emergency	panicking
fiery	prehistoric
horrifying	scientific
immediately	within

TARGET STRATEGY **Summarize** Tell the important parts of the text in your own words.

Word Teaser Which word is the opposite of later?